FROM FACTORY TO TABLE
WHAT YOU'RE REALLY EATING™

THE TRUTH BEHIND
GMOS

KATHARINA SMUNDAK

rosen publishing's
rosen
central

New York

Published in 2018 by The Rosen Publishing Group, Inc.
29 East 21st Street, New York, NY 10010

Copyright © 2018 by The Rosen Publishing Group, Inc.

First Edition

Library of Congress Cataloging-in-Publication Data

Names: Smundak, Katharina, author.
Title: The truth behind GMOs / Katharina Smundak.
Description: New York : Rosen Central, 2018. | Series: From factory to table: what you're really eating | Audience: Grades 5-8. | Includes bibliographical references and index.
Identifiers: LCCN 2017019021| ISBN 9781499439298 (library bound) | ISBN 9781499439274 (pbk.) | ISBN 9781499439281 (6 pack)
Subjects: LCSH: Transgenic organisms—Juvenile literature. | Crops—Genetic engineering—Juvenile literature. | Agricultural biotechnology—Juvenile literature.
Classification: LCC QH442.6 .S68 2018 | DDC 338.1/7—dc23
LC record available at https://lccn.loc.gov/2017019021

Manufactured in China

CONTENTS

Many of us grew up far from farms and most of us buy food at the grocery store or super-market, where it is already packaged. We do not pick our apples off the tree, we do not dig the potatoes we eat out of the ground, so it is easy not to think about where our food comes from and how it is grown. Food is grown by farmers who have the task of feeding a growing world population. While our population grows, our resources remain the same. Today, an important question facing farmers, but also governments, and ultimately, humans, is: how do we increase food production?

The use of genetically modified crops is one of the answers currently provided to the question of how to increase food production. Genetically modified plants are often referred to as GMOs. "GMO" stands for "genetically modified organism," and it refers to plants whose DNA has been modified by adding genes from different organisms. The primary goal of these modifications is to increase crop yield: the quantity of food we can eat created by the planted crop. Most GM crops are designed to be resistant to pesticides or toxic to pests like bacteria or viruses. Plants have also been modified to be drought resistant or to produce vitamins they don't naturally produce.

It is natural for people to worry about the food they put in their bodies, and many people are frightened by GMOs because they consider them unnatural. The fact is that GMOs are subject to a lot of testing before they are sold as food. Thousands of studies and hundreds of thousands of meals later, there is no evidence that GMOs are harmful to humans. Still, they

Usually, we don't get our apples straight from the tree. We buy them in the store without knowing exactly where they came from or how they were grown.

remain controversial. In order to be informed, we should understand the reasons why GMOs exist. An informed eater should also be familiar with the arguments against GMO use, some of which are valid and worth considering, while others are based on fear and not on evidence.

The use of GM crops does raise important questions about our agricultural practices, which rely heavily on the use of pesticides and fertilizer. Although they perform important functions, fertilizer and pesticides have negative consequences for our environment and for our health. While

There is a lot of misinformation about GMOs. Many people think they are unsafe, and many food companies have started labeling their foods as non-GMO.

GM crops are not dangerous themselves, they are part of a system that is currently not sustainable and that bears reevaluation. What can we do to better manage our resources? How can we avoid damaging the environment we live in while still producing the food we need? What practices can we put into place that will allow us to keep feeding the planet in the long term?

CHAPTER ONE

WHAT ARE GMOS ANYWAY?

Maybe you've heard the term "GMO" on the news, or maybe you've seen an article about it, or you've heard people you know and even politicians talking about it. So what is a GMO? A GMO is a genetically modified organism. That term can apply to a lot of different things and it's not very precise, but most of the time when people say GMO, they are referring to plants whose DNA has been modified for the plant to exhibit a certain quality, like pest resistance. A more accurate term is "transgenic" because genetic material from one organism has been transferred to another.

BUT FIRST, SOME HISTORY

Humans have been "genetically modifying" plants for thousands of years through artificial selection. Imagine a farmer plants tomatoes and among his tomato plants, one yields many more tomatoes than the others. The farmer wants to grow as many tomatoes as possible, so the next season, he plants seeds only from that very productive tomato plant.

Whatever makes that one plant more productive is encoded in its DNA. The other tomato plants from that field don't get to pass on their DNA to the next generation. Instead, only the DNA of the plant chosen by the farmer is passed on. So, by choosing and planting variations of plants that exhibited desirable qualities farmers were, in fact, genetically modifying plants. These desirable qualities are traits encoded in genes, although farmers of the past didn't know that. This method of breeding plants is called artificial selection or selective breeding.

Eventually, starting in the nineteenth century, scientists began understanding how genes were inherited. Over the course of the twentieth century, scientists made the connection between physical traits and DNA. They realized that genes are DNA code for certain qualities, and eventually they were able to isolate these genes. Once that was possible, those genes could be inserted into the DNA of other organisms. For example, if you have diabetes and you need insulin, it is very likely that the insulin you buy as medication was actually produced by *E. coli* bacteria! Scientists found the genetic code that was responsible for the creation

of insulin and inserted it into bacterial DNA. Since genes are the code to create, or synthesize, proteins, these bacteria now had the tools to synthesize insulin, which is a protein.

Farmers have been trying to grow the best crops for thousands of years. Now, science has stepped in to make it easier.

Transgenic plants are created using the same principle as that used to create insulin. Say you find an organism, like a bacterium, that can kill a particular insect. This insect loves eating corn, so you want your corn to be resistant to this insect, just

JELLYFISH AND TRANSGENES!

Also called the crystal jellyfish, the *Aequorea victoria* is bioluminescent.

Inserting DNA from one organism into another is called transformation. A basic experiment in biotechnology to demonstrate how DNA, genes, and proteins are linked involves a glow-in-the-dark protein called green fluorescent protein (GFP), which was extracted from a deep sea jellyfish, the *Aequorea victoria*. A circular piece of DNA, called the plasmid, is inserted into bacteria. This particular plasmid, called pGLO, has the genetic code for GFP. If the bacteria have been successfully transformed, the bacteria will start glowing in the dark. In biotechnology, GFP is used to make sure that another gene, whose expression is not visible, has been absorbed in DNA.

like that bacteria. You examine the bacteria's DNA, find the gene responsible for this insect resistance and then insert it into the DNA of one corn cell. Eventually, your one corn cell will divide into two, those cells will divide, too, and so on, until finally you have a plant that is resistant to that insect. That corn is transgenic corn, though you'll generally hear it called GMO corn.

Corn is one of the biggest crops in the United States. Farmers use transgenic corn to increase their yields.

GMOS: BAD APPLES?

The reason you may have heard about GMO plants is because a lot of people think that GMOs are dangerous to our health. Genetically engineered (GE) seeds were introduced in 1996, and since then many studies have been undertaken to investigate their potential to harm. More than two thousand of them have concluded that GMOs are not harmful to humans. The American Medical Association, the National Academy of Sciences, and the British Royal Academy, among other scientific organizations, have stated that GE food is not more dangerous than any other food. The European Union (EU) is composed of member states who oppose the use of GMOs. Even there, its scientists released a report called "A Decade of EU-funded GMO Research," in which they said, "The main conclusion to be drawn from the efforts of more than 130 research projects, covering a period of more than 25 years of research and involving more than 500 independent research groups, is that biotechnology, and in particular GMOs, are not per se more risky than e.g. conventional plant breeding technologies." In addition, all GE foods are tested on animals before coming to market, a practice we do not use with conventionally bred crops.

If GE food were bad for us, there would be cases of people getting sick as a result of eating it, but there haven't been any that directly linked the two. Not only that, there haven't been cases of animals getting sick because of GE food. In 2014, University of California-Davis Department of Animal Science geneticist Alison Van Eenennaam and research assistant Amy E. Young reviewed livestock health and productivity over twenty-nine years, from before and after the introduction of GMO animal feed, in an article called "Prevalence and Impacts of Genetically Engineered Feedstuffs on Livestock Populations." They write,

United States animal agriculture produces over 9 billion food-producing animals annually, and more than 95% of these animals consume feed containing GE ingredients. Data on livestock productivity and health were collated from publicly available sources from 1983, before the introduction of GE crops in 1996, and subsequently through 2011, a period with high levels of predominately GE animal feed. These field data sets, representing over 100 billion animals following the introduction of GE crops, did not reveal unfavorable or perturbed trends in livestock health and productivity. No study has revealed any differences in the nutritional profile of animal products derived from GE-fed animals.

In other words, although billions of animals have eaten trillions of meals containing GE ingredients, their health now compared to their health prior to the introduction of GE feed has not been affected. There were no differences in the health of animals that ate GE ingredients and those that did not.

Once you understand that transgenic plants are just a more precise way of doing what humans have been doing for thousands of years—making plants inherit and exhibit desirable traits—it makes sense that they are not harmful. In the past, a farmer wanted a more productive crop so he would choose the plant that was most productive, though he didn't know what made it so. Now, scientists are able to identify the genes responsible for elements of productivity. The idea is the same, but the methods are not. That being said, GE food does have some negative indirect effects on our environment and on our health, which will be addressed after we've explored how GMOs are used.

MYTH

GMOs are bad for your health.

FACT

There has been no proof after twenty years of testing that GMOs themselves have negative impacts on the health of humans who eat them.

MYTH

GMOs are all developed and sold by corporations like Monsanto and DuPont.

FACT

Although the most commonly used GE seeds are sold by Monsanto and DuPont, nonprofits like the International Rice Research Institute as well as public universities have also been researching and developing GE seeds.

MYTH

GMOs have caused an increase in the use of pesticides.

FACT

There are two dominant GE crop types. One that causes the plant to express a protein that is toxic to insects and another that makes the plant resistant to a type of pesticide called glyphosate. The first trait has made it possible to reduce insecticide use, while the second does encourage the use of an herbicide, but one that is much less toxic that previously used ones.

CHAPTER TWO

WHY DO WE USE GMO CROPS?

Let's remember the primary purpose of farming: to grow the food that feeds us. But Earth's population is growing. Just think: at the beginning of the twentieth century, there were 1.65 billion people on Earth. By 2011, the world population had reached 7 billion! But the size of the planet hasn't changed since then. We have the same amount of resources as before, but we need to share them among a growing number of people. As of 2005, according to *National Geographic*, about half the earth's land is being used for food production: either for crops or for feeding livestock. And don't forget: we still need space to live and for other activities. So one of the challenges before us is: how do we extract more out of the land we have since we can't just keep finding more land to cultivate?

The population may be growing but Earth is not. There is limited space to grow food.

A KIND OF GREEN REVOLUTION

Improved irrigation, better weather monitoring, crop rotation, synthetic fertilizers, and high-yielding seed varieties have all made the production of the amount of food we need to feed us possible. This collection of new technologies and methods was promoted by scientists and governments in a movement called the Green Revolution. Though research began in the 1930s, it is in the 1960s that it really took off. The intent behind the Green Revolution was to prevent world hunger.

The Green Revolution was designed to introduce new technologies, tools, and methods to agriculture in order to increase food production. One method was double-cropping: growing two crops per season on existing farmland. Irrigation projects, like dams, made double-cropping possible, so farmers didn't have to just rely on the rainy season. Another way to increase food production was using high-yield seed varieties, of wheat and rice in particular. The Green Revolution was a big success in Mexico, Pakistan, and India. In India, for example, prior to the Green Revolution, wheat was imported. Because of the Green Revolution, India became an occasional net exporter of wheat, meaning it exported more wheat than it imported. According to Jesse Ausubel and others in the article "Peak Farmland and the Prospect for Land Sparing" (2012), without Green Revolution technology, India would have had to cultivate 65 million hectares (160 million acres) to get the same result. That's an area the size of France! In the United States, according to the report "Major Uses of Land in the United States, 2007" published by the United States Department of Agriculture's Economic Research Service, total cropland has been declining since 1978. It has declined 10 percent between 2007

WHAT ARE HIGH-YIELD SEEDS?

High-yield seeds are varieties of plant seeds that have a higher than average yield. Norman Borlaug, for example, was an American biologist responsible for the creation of high-yielding "dwarf" wheat. Through artificial selection, Borlaug developed wheat in which most of the energy (and remember, we eat food for fuel) was stored in the kernel and not in the stalk, which is inedible. As a result, you could get more grain per acre. Basically, you get more food and use less land to get it. It was this wheat that was planted in India and that allowed the country to become a wheat exporter.

and 1945: from 451 million acres (182 million ha) to 408 million acres (165 million ha), an area roughly the size of Mississippi or Florida.

Something similar happened to rice. In 1966, the International Rice Research Institute (IRRI) developed a strain of rice through crossbreeding called IR8. Thanks to IR8, rice yield went from about two tons per hectare to roughly ten (though that number has since fallen). In "The Next Green Revolution" published in *National Geographic*, Tom Folger writes, "From the 1960s through the 1990s, yields of rice and wheat in Asia doubled. Even as the continent's population increased by 60

Figuring out how to grow more food is key to making sure everyone is fed. Rice is one crop that has benefited from scientific discoveries.

percent, grain prices fell, the average Asian consumed nearly a third more calories, and the poverty rate was cut in half."

Although the Green Revolution greatly improved the efficiency of food production, the seed varieties it promoted also relied on the heavy use of synthetic fertilizers and pesticides to produce their high yields. IR8, for example, requires nitrogen fertilizer to trigger its short growth duration and high yield. Both fertilizers and pesticides have many negative effects: they are harmful, and at times deadly, to animals, to humans, and to whole ecosystems, including our oceans. As you can see, we have a problem: on one hand, we need to produce food on a massive scale for a growing population and we have limited resources, like water and land, to do so. On the other hand, the high-yield seeds and the fertilizer and pesticides they demand are toxic.

CLEANING UP OUR MESS

GE plants provide one possible solution to this issue. Currently, the most common transgenic crops are corn, cotton, and soybeans. Two of the most desirable traits in transgenic crops are insect resistance and herbicide tolerance. The DNA of insect-resistant plants includes a gene that makes the plants produce a protein that is toxic to certain insects. Cotton and corn that is resistant to insects is called Bt cotton and corn, respectively (there are no insect-resistant varieties of soybeans). Herbicide-tolerant (HT) crops are engineered to be resistant to the herbicide glyphosate, whose brand name is Roundup. This resistance allows the crops to be sprayed with glyphosate to kill weeds growing around the crop without killing the crop itself. Glyphosate is an herbicide that is less toxic than other herbicides in use. Writing for *Nature* in "Case Studies: A Hard Look at GM Crops," Natasha Gilbert cites a study by PG Economics, which said that the use of HT cotton had decreased the use of herbicide by 15.5 million kilograms (34 million pounds) between 1996 and 2011. As of 2016, according to the USDA Economic Research group, in the United States, 93 percent of cotton, 94 percent of soybeans, and 92 percent of corn acreage is either Bt, HT, or both.

Pest resistance reduces the need for pesticides. According to the USDA, since the introduction of Bt corn, pesticide use has fallen 90 percent. Similarly, in "Seeds of Doubt," a *New Yorker* article, Michael Specter cites a study by the International Food Policy Research Institute on the introduction of Bt cotton in India: "Bt farmers spend at least 15 percent more on crops, but their pesticide costs are 50 percent lower. Since the seed was introduced, yields have increased by more than 150 percent."

Another desirable quality for farmers is virus resistance. A plant virus is a virus with the ability to hurt plants and sometimes kill them. Papaya fruit in Hawaii, for example, were being killed by the papaya ringspot virus (PRSV). Between 1992, when PRSV was discovered in Puna, Hawaii (where the majority of Hawaiian papaya was grown), and 1998, papaya production fell from 53

Here you can see papayas growing on a farm. With the introduction of the Rainbow papaya, papayas are no longer at risk for ringspot.

million pounds (24 million kg) to 26 million pounds (11 million kg). That's basically half! The introduction of a virus-resistant papaya, called the Rainbow papaya, allowed papaya production to climb back up to 40 million pounds (18 million kg) by 2001.

Our food supply is also being affected by climate change. Climate change is bringing with it more droughts, which affect crops since crops depend on rainfall. For the moment, both Monsanto, a seed-distributing corporation, as well as agricultural projects are working on developing corn that will be able to produce in droughts. This work is happening in conjunction with traditional crossbreeding methods.

Golden rice contains beta-carotene, an important nutrient also found in carrots.

Finally, some transgenic seeds have functions not connected to their survival. Transgenic crops can also have traits that will benefit the person eating them, like golden rice. Golden rice is a transgenic crop still in development. It contains beta-carotene. When we eat foods containing beta-carotene, like squash or carrots, it turns into vitamin A in our bodies. If you are vitamin A deficient, you do not have enough of the vitamin in your body. In her article "Golden Rice: Lifesaver?" published in the *New York Times,* Amy Harmon writes that vitamin A deficiency causes blindness in a quarter million to a half million children in the world. It also makes your immune system weak, causing the deaths of some two million people every year.

CHAPTER THREE

WHAT'S ALL THE FUSS ABOUT?

Although GMOs have beneficial functions, they are still fairly controversial. Some countries, like India, ban the cultivation of GE food crops. Others ban GE cultivation with some exceptions—for example, France, Germany, Italy, and other European Union countries—while still others ban both their cultivation and import, like Russia. In the United States, which grows the most GE crops in the world, there have been several proposals to mandate labeling of GE foods as a warning to consumers.

HONEY, I SHRUNK OUR BIODIVERSITY

One of the biggest problems with GE crops is reduced biodiversity. Biodiversity is the variety of living things in an environment, be it the size of the earth or something much smaller, like your own backyard. The United Nations Food and Agriculture Organization reports that 75 percent of plant genetic diversity has been lost since 1900. Instead of planting local varieties of crops that are best adapted to

EXAMPLES OF REDUCED BIODIVERSITY

A famous historical case of the consequences of a lack of diversity in plants was the Irish potato blight. In the 1800s, farmers in Ireland were planting the same potato variety, the Irish Lumper, and when an organism started attacking these potatoes, it wiped out the potato supply, which was a major food source. The result was the Irish Potato Famine, which killed a million people and pushed a million more to emigrate.

A similar phenomenon occurred and is occurring with the banana. Until the 1960s, the overwhelming majority of bananas eaten in the world were Gros Michel bananas, until a fungus called Panama disease destroyed the crop. The banana we eat now—and it accounts for 99 percent of the bananas grown in the world—is called the Cavendish. Now, fifty years after its introduction as a banana resistant to Panama disease, it, too, is falling victim to a fungus called tropical race 4.

DEPARTURE OF THE "NIMROD" AND "ATHLONE" STEAMERS, WITH EMIGRANTS ON BOARD, FOR LIVERPOOL.

The Irish Potato Famine forced millions of Irish to leave their country. Many sailed across the Atlantic Ocean to the United States.

their environments, farmers have chosen and governments have encouraged the growth of high-yield, genetically uniform crops. We know why farmers choose these crops: they are reliably productive. The problem is that if a disease or a pest were to attack one of these types of crops, the whole planted crop—and consequently a part of our food supply—would be affected because that whole crop has the same DNA and so would be uniformly susceptible to it.

PRISON BREAK

Another cause for concern is what's known as transgene escape or introgression, which is the idea that transgenic crops will cross with wild plants and create plants growing in the wild with transgenes in their DNA. In "Transgene Introgression from Genetically Modified Crops to Their Wild Relatives," published in *Nature*, C. Neal Stewart, Matthew D. Halfhill, and Suzanne I. Warwick discuss the potential for this outcome. They conclude that for some GM crops, this outcome is unlikely, but they do warn that some GM crops, like sunflower, canola, and sorghum, are at high risk of hybridizing, or breeding, with their wild relatives. The biggest fear is that the GM versions will pass herbicide tolerance to their wild relatives, which would make those relatives harder to kill and as a result make the GM crop harder to grow since the wild relative is unwanted and acts like a weed. Remember, weeds are just plants that we don't want. They are not problematic in and of themselves, they are just made problematic if they do not coincide with the grower's goals. That said, panic about the possibility of these "transgenic weeds" is much higher than its actual likelihood, though careful testing and consideration of this outcome should always be carried out with every GE product.

WHEN TOLERANCE IS NOT DESIRABLE

A bigger issue with regard to weeds is herbicide tolerance caused by the use of HT crops. However, in the case of HT crops, because farmers are spraying their crops with glyphosate only, weeds that are not killed by the herbicide become resistant to it. Glyphosate-resistant weeds have been found in at least eighteen countries. This resistance requires farmers to spray even more herbicide, thus creating a vicious cycle. Already, a study by David Mortensen from Pennsylvania State University estimates that herbicide use will rise from 1.5 kilograms (3.3 pounds) in 2013 to 3.5 kilograms (7.7 pounds) per hectare (2.4 acres) by 2025 due to GE crop use. Such an outcome will make the benefits of HT crops null. Due to glyphosate resistance, other herbicides will have to be introduced into the pesticide cocktail along with developing more sustainable farming practices. It is important to remember, however, that herbicide resistance develops in weeds regardless of whether or not they plant GM crops. Resistant weeds grow around plants bred through conventional methods and sprayed with herbicides. In fact, the first glyphosate-resistant weeds were found in Australia in 1996, a country that did not grow GM crops at all! As Andrew Kniss, a weed scientist at the University of Wyoming, writes on his blog Weed Control Freaks, "Herbicide resistant weed development is not a GMO problem, it is a herbicide problem."

Insect resistance is another issue. GE crops resistant to insects are created by inserting genes from the *Bacillus thuringiensis* (Bt), a bacterium that codes for proteins that are toxic to insects but not toxic to humans. Insect tolerance works in the same way as herbicide tolerance: those insects that are Bt toler-

Creating herbicide-resistant weeds is a consequence of HT crops. This is similar to what happens with bacteria. Any bacteria not killed by antibiotics may become drug resistant.

ant survive, those that aren't die, and so the Bt-tolerant trait gets passed down to future generations. To avoid this issue, the EPA requires farmers to plant refuges, which are areas next to fields planted with non-GE varieties of the crop. Refuges allow insects that are not Bt resistant to mate with resistant insects, thereby decreasing the likelihood of resistant offspring.

WHOSE SEEDS ARE THESE ANYWAY?

Genetically engineered seeds are controversial, too, because, particularly with corn, cotton, and soybeans, they have been developed and are sold exclusively by the companies that produce them. According to a report by the ETC group, three corporations—Monsanto, DuPont Pioneer, and Syngenta—control 60 percent of the market. These companies have developed the seeds and patented them. Patents are ways of protecting new ideas, also known as intellectual property. The idea is that thoughts are also property, like a bicycle, and just as it's illegal to steal someone's bike, it is illegal to steal someone's idea. These patents for the genetically engineered seeds allow companies to make back the money they invested into developing a product. On its website, Monsanto says that it spends $2.6 million a day on research and development.

As a result, when farmers buy seeds from these companies, they sign an agreement not to replant these seeds. They must buy new seeds every year. Farmers are thus dependent on the companies for seeds. Farmers are dependent on these companies in other ways as well: in the case of HT crops, the herbicide is created and sold by the same company, Monsanto, as the seed itself. Patents, however, are temporary. Already, the patent for Roundup, the glyphosate herbicide used with HT seeds, has expired and competitors have come out. The patent for Roundup Ready Soy has also already expired. The University of Arkansas offers free, replantable Roundup Ready Soy seeds. Moreover, there are other staple crops whose development is not controlled by these corporations. Wheat, for example, is largely developed by universities in the United States. The golden rice previously mentioned would cost about as much as regular rice. The aforementioned Rainbow papaya was developed by academic and government researchers. Monsanto, DuPont, and Syngenta play big roles in developing corn, soybeans, and cotton, but their research does not extend to many other staple crops, like cassava, potatoes, and rice, among others.

Patented seeds make farmers dependent on large corporations for their livelihoods. There have been cases of farmers being sued for using seeds without permission.

Of course, genetically engineered seeds are more expensive than others. Though these seeds are more expensive, farmers buy them nonetheless because they save money elsewhere. In "Seeds of Doubt," Michael Specter cites the International Food Policy Research Institute, which reported that Bt cotton farmers in India spent 15 percent more on the seeds themselves but saved 50 percent on pesticides, and yields increased 150 percent. Clearly, for farmers there is a reason to choose genetically engineered crops, even though these choices do reduce seed diversity.

Finally, some people are against GE crops because they consider them unnatural. It is common to see human intervention in

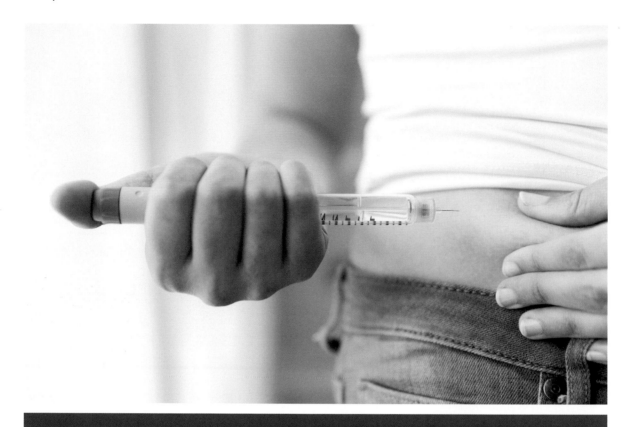

Many seemingly unnatural scientific advancements have saved millions of lives, including insulin, which helps people with diabetes lead normal lives.

genetics as "playing God." The idea of taking DNA from one organism and inserting it into another seems wrong. And yet, people have no problem with bacteria producing insulin or with doctors using pig valves in human hearts, a routine surgical practice.

Much of the debate surrounding GE seeds is grounded in emotion and not in actual danger. More than two thousand studies have concluded that GE crops in and of themselves are not dangerous for human consumption. However, GE crops play an important part in industrial agriculture, which is genuinely problematic.

CHAPTER FOUR

THE ROOT OF THE PROBLEM

Some of the accusations made against GE seeds are valid, but they are equally valid for non-GE seeds. Some people say that the use of HT crops creates the conditions for herbicide-resistant weeds to grow. But as we've seen, the problem is not the seeds themselves, but rather the use of one kind of herbicide, glyphosate. Indeed, GE seeds themselves are not the issue. Rather, it is the system that they are a part of that is the problem. GE seeds provide solutions to important agricultural problems, like pests and viruses, but these problems exist only because of the use of monoculture in industrial agriculture. Mono-cropping creates issues that GE seeds resolve without addressing the root issue. GE seeds enable the continuation of monocropping, and that is why they are problematic.

Monocropping is the practice of planting a single crop in a given large area every year. Since the Green Revolution, monocropping, in combination with the use of synthetic fertilizers, has allowed farmers to increase their yields without expanding the land on which they cultivate. When farmers plant only one crop, a monoculture, they do not have to adjust the depth at which they plant the seed; different seeds should be planted at different depths. They can use the same pesticide for the whole field, they can harvest more easily as the crops grow to a uniform height, and they don't have to sort through the harvest to separate out the different products. Basically, monoculture allows farmers to mechanize the farming process, from planting to harvest. Mechanization frees up a lot of people from working in farming.

Monocropping—a monoculture over time—would not be possible without the use of synthetic fertilizers. They play a key role in increasing productivity by providing plants with nutrients that promote growth, the most important of which are nitrogen,

We do not have everything figured out yet. While monocropping has made many things easier for farmers, it has also caused many problems that need to be addressed.

phosphorus, and potassium. Monocropping makes farmers very dependent on fertilizers since planting one crop on the same land depletes that land of the nutrients that plants need. In addition, when farmers do not plant anything in a field to let the soil "rest" and to avoid having to clear weeds when they decide to plant in that field, they also prevent the buildup of nutrients in the soil since there are no plants to feed it and to maintain it. Changing the crops planted on a given area every couple of years, a process called crop rotation, allows other crops to deposit in the soil the nutrients that the other crops remove. So, for example, while corn uses nitrogen from the soil, soy deposits nitrogen in the soil. Rotating the two crops helps replace the nutrients that the crops consume. While crop rotation allows for the replacement of nitrogen, adding other nutrients is more complicated. Phosphorus is an essential plant nutrient, for example. However, its sources are limited, so in the future, we will have to consider the use of feces as a source of phosphorus. Another option for decreasing fertilizer use is polyculture: planting multiple crops at the same time. Polyculture, however, demands more workers in the field. In any case, according to Andrew McGuire of Washington State University's Center for Sustaining Agriculture and Resources, ending the use of synthetic fertilizer is very unlikely, though it is still possible to reduce its use through better farming practices.

Not only does monocropping force an overreliance on synthetic fertilizer, it also leads to an increase in pests and diseases. If a pest finds a crop it likes to feed on, it will stay in that area. If that crop is rotated with another crop that the pest does not eat, then it will die. To fight the pests that monocultures introduce, farmers have to use pesticides to kill them. Monocropping can also increase disease since it can spread from one plant to another, so farmers have to rely on disease-resistant plant varieties. As we know, disease resistance does not last forever, nor

HOW WILL WE FEED ALL THESE PEOPLE?

Nitrogen is essential for plants to grow and is a very important factor in crop productivity. In general, without nitrogen, you don't have life! It plays a big part in photosynthesis, the conversion of sunlight into energy; it is also an essential component in amino acids, which are the building blocks of proteins. Without proteins, plants die. Some plants, like wheat, get nitrogen from the soil. Nitrogen can also be found in manure and in guano—bat feces. It comprises 80 percent of our air! But plants cannot take nitrogen directly from the air.

By the end of the nineteenth century, people started thinking that we had reached peak agricultural capacity: crops couldn't be made any more productive and so people would not be able to be fed. But at the turn of the twentieth century, Fritz Haber, a German scientist, working with his assistant Robert Rossignol, discovered a way to convert the nitrogen in the air into ammonia by combining it with hydrogen under extreme pressure at high heat in a metal tank. This discovery is called the Haber-Bosch process. Ammonia is a liquid that could be applied to plants. In fact, it is a synthetic fertilizer, the invention of which has allowed our planet's population to grow to its current size. Today, we use one hundred million tons of synthetic fertilizer every year.

are pesticides forever effective as resistance develops. Pesticides and synthetic fertilizers are expenses for farmers that keep increasing as the development of pest resistance increases the need for pesticides and the depletion of soil nutrients forces increased use of fertilizers. Both of these products are bad for the environment and for us.

Though the reliance on pesticides and synthetic fertilizer began before the creation of GE seeds, GE seeds contribute further to the already problematic monocropping system. Of course, planting thousands of acres of organic corn year after year would also lead to an increase in pests and disease: GE seeds are not the cause of the problem; they are a response to it. In fact, the most highly sought after qualities in GE seeds—pesticide resistance and pest resistance—address problems created by monocropping. The controversy shouldn't be around GE seeds themselves since they are not harmful to our heath. It should be around some of the major reasons for their development and their contribution to an agricultural system that is unsustainable.

ONE CROP TO RULE THEM ALL

Another issue is the type of GE seeds that are used. So far, soy and corn have been the most widely planted GE crops. Corn and soy are being grown very efficiently, but what are they being used for? In an interview in the *Washington Post*, McKay Jenkins, the author of *Food Fight: GMOs and the Future of the American Diet*, says that corn and soybeans end up as ingredients in our processed foods: corn, in the form of high-fructose corn syrup, and both corn and soy in the food fed to the animals that become the processed meat sold by fast food restaurants (among others). These foods are directly linked with obesity and its accompanying problems: diabetes, high blood pressure, and some cancers. Keep in mind, though: it's not the fact that they are GE that makes corn and soy bad for you!

What solutions are there, then, to the issues of modern industrial agriculture? It seems clear that monocropping is not a practice we can rely on. Crop rotation in and of itself would reduce the use of pesticides and synthetic fertilizer, and it would decrease the development of pesticide-resistant organisms. Polyculture, while beneficial for the soil, does not necessarily create the same yields as monoculture: this is a subject of debate.

There is some form of corn in many processed foods, particularly corn syrup. Corn syrup is used to sweeten just about everything!

It is also important to rethink the crops that we are planting: is it necessary for the United States to grow as much corn as it does when so much of it—either directly or indirectly—goes toward producing food that is bad for us? In this sense, GE crops play a negative role.

Yet because GE crops are not risky in and of themselves, they can contribute, along with other practices, to resolving a fundamental challenge for humanity: feeding a growing population sustainably so that we do not use up the limited resources we have on Earth. Maybe GE seeds, such as golden rice, will help us deal with health problems, or maybe they will allow us to grow food in a changing climate that is more susceptible to droughts. In any case, we should focus on practices that won't deplete our resources. We cannot continue to rely on pesticides and synthetic fertilizer to grow our food. The role of GE seeds is a problem insofar as it helps continue that system. But if GE crops can help us find an answer to feeding our population, there is nothing wrong with that. As McKay Jenkins said in the *Washington Post*: "The goal is sustainability. The goal is not some kind of purity."

10 GREAT QUESTIONS
TO ASK A NUTRITIONIST

1. How can I avoid misinformation about what's healthy for me?

2. Are organic foods healthier?

3. How can I support local farmers?

4. What should I eat to make sure I have a balanced diet?

5. How does misinformation about food safety get started?

6. Are there any types of food I should avoid?

7. How do I know if I'm healthy?

8. Are there any other foods that are thought to be unsafe that aren't really?

9. Should I eat less processed food?

10. Are all fruits and vegetables genetically modified in some way?

GLOSSARY

artificial selection The process of deliberately crossing plants or animals to develop desirable characteristics, or traits, in future generations. This process is also referred to as selective breeding.

biodiversity The variety of life in a particular ecosystem, habitat, or the world at large.

crop rotation The practice of changing planted crops year after year. For contrast, see monocropping.

crossbreeding Breeding an organism with an organism from another species, breed, or variety.

fertilizer A material used on soil or on plants to provide plants with necessary nutrients for growth, among them nitrogen, phosphate, and potassium.

genetically engineered (GE) Refers to an organism whose DNA has been changed with the addition of DNA from another organism.

glyphosate A type of pesticide, often known by its brand name, Roundup.

monocropping In agriculture, the practice of planting the same crop in an area year after year.

patent Temporary ownership of an idea granted to an inventor by the government to protect the idea from theft.

pesticide A substance that prevents, repels, or destroys pests, which can come in the form of insects, weeds, fungi, and rodents. Correspondingly, pesticides can be insecticides, herbicides, fungicides, or rodenticides.

polyculture The practice of planting multiple crops at the same time on a given area. For contrast, see monoculture.

resistance The natural ability of an organism to survive or avoid a substance that is toxic to it.

yield The quantity of something, like a crop, produced.

Bill and Melinda Gates Foundation
440 5th Avenue North
Seattle, WA 98109
(206) 709-3100 ext. 7100
Website: http://www.gatesfoundation.org
Facebook: @gatesfoundation
Twitter: @gatesfoundation
The Bill and Melinda Gates Foundation is interested in reducing famine and food insecurity in sub-Saharan African and in Southeast Asia and gives money for solutions that involve GM crops. It has given funding to the IRRI, for example.

Canada Food Inspection Agency (CFIA)
1400 Merivale Road
Ottawa, ON K1A 0Y9
Canada
(800) 442-2342
Website: http://www.inspection.gc.ca
Facebook: @CFIACanada
Twitter: @CFIA_Canada
The CFIA maintains and enforces food standards that will benefit people, animals, and the environment.

Center for Sustaining Agriculture and Natural Resources at Washington State University
2606 W. Pioneer
Puyallup, WA 98371
(509) 663-8181 ext. 265
Website: http://www.csanr.wsu.edu
Facebook: @CSANR
This university department is devoted to improving sustainability. Their site provides information on issues in agriculture.

Environmental Protection Agency (EPA)
1200 Pennsylvania Avenue NW
Washington, DC 20460
(202) 272-0167
Website: http://www.epa.gov
Facebook: @EPA
Twitter: @EPA
The EPA provides helpful and easy to understand information on
    US government policies concerning the effects of pollutants,
    like pesticides, on our environment.

International Food Policy Research Institute (IFPRI)
2033 K Street NW
Washington, DC 20006
(202) 862-5600
Website: http://www.ifpri.org
Twitter: @IFPRI
IFPRI is an organization that researches policies that could be
    put into place in order to introduce sustainable practices to
    end malnutrition and hunger. Its site has useful information on
    GM use in the world.

International Rice Research Institute (IRRI)
DAPO Box 7777
Metro Manila 1301
Philippines
+63 2 580 5600
Website: http://www.irri.org
Facebook: @IRRI.ricenews
Twitter: @RiceResearch
This nonprofit has played an important role in the development of
    various strains of rice, a staple crop in much of the world. It is
    also responsible for the development of golden rice.

United States Department of Agriculture (USDA)
1400 Independence Avenue SW
Washington, DC 20250
(202) 720-2791
Website: http://www.usda.gov
Facebook: @USDA
Twitter: @USDA
The USDA is the branch of the US government responsible for setting agricultural policy in the United States and making sure that food production in the United States remains sustainable. It is a good resource for learning about current uses for GM crops.

WEBSITES

Because of the changing nature of internet links, Rosen Publishing has developed an online list of websites related to the subject of this book. This site is updated regularly. Please use this link to access the list:

http://www.rosenlinks.com/FFTT/GMO

FOR FURTHER READING

Barber, Dan. *The Third Plate: Field Notes on the Future of Food*. New York, NY: Penguin Books, 2015.

Brasch, Nicolas. *The Foods We Eat* (The Science Behind). Mankato, MN: Smart Apple Media, 2010.

Centore, Michael. *Genetically Modified Foods*. Broomall, PA : Mason Crest, 2017.

Colson, Mary. *GMOs* (Cutting-Edge Technology). New York, NY: Gareth Stevens Publishing, 2017.

Forman, Lillian E. *Genetically Modified Foods*. Edina, MN: ABDO Publishing, 2010.

Gardner, Jane P. *Food Science* (Science 24/7). Broomall, PA: Mason Crest, 2016.

Gay, Kathlyn. *Superfood or Superthreat: The Issue of Genetically Engineered Food* (Issues in Focus Today). Berkeley Heights, NJ: Enslow, 2008.

Hand, Carol. *Sustainable Agriculture*. Minneapolis, MN: Essential Library, an imprint of Abdo Publishing, 2016.

Hesser, Leon. *The Man Who Fed the World*. Dallas, TX: Durban House Publishing, 2006.

Jenkins, McKay. *Food Fight: GMOs and the Future of the American Diet*. New York, NY: Penguin RandomHouse, 2017.

Rissman, Rebecca. *Genetically Modified Food* (Food Matters). Minneapolis, MN: Core Library, 2016.

Anderson, Teresa. "GM Agriculture Is Not the Answer to Seed Diversity—It's Part of the Problem." *Guardian*, October 17, 2013. https://www.theguardian.com/global-development /poverty-matters/2013/oct/17/gm-agriculture-not-answer -seed-diversity.

Ausubel, J. H., I. K. Wernick, and P. E. Waggoner. "Peak Farmland and the Prospect for Land Sparing." *Population and Development Review*, 38 (2013): 221–242. doi:10.1111/j.1728 -4457.2013.00561.x.

Borel, Brooke. "GMO Facts: 10 Common GMO Claims Debunked." *Popular Science*, July 11, 2014. http://www.popsci.com/article /science/core-truths-10-common-gmo-claims-debunked.

Dewey, Caitlin. "We're Having the Wrong Argument about GMOs." *Washington Post*, February 6, 2017. https://www .washingtonpost.com/news/wonk/wp/2017/02/06/were-having -the-wrong-argument-about-gmos.

Entine, Joe. "The Debate About GMO Safety Is Over, Thanks to a New Trillion-Meal Study." Forbes.com, September 17, 2014. https://www.forbes.com/sites/jonentine/2014/09/17/the-debate -about-gmo-safety-is-over-thanks-to-a-new-trillion-meal-study /#1278c5668a63.

European Commission. "A Decade of EU-Funded GMO Research." Luxembourg: Publications Office of the European Union, 2010. doi 10.2777/97784.

Ferman, Roberto A. "Bye, Bye, Bananas." *Washington Post*, December 5, 2014. https://www.washingtonpost.com/news /wonk/wp/2015/12/04/the-worlds-most-popular-banana-could -go-extinct.

Fermin, G., P. Tennant, C. Gonsalves, D. Lee, and D. Gonsalves. "Comparative Development and Impact of Transgenic Papayas in Hawaii, Jamaica, and Venezuela," in Pena, L., ed. *Transgenic Plants: Methods and Protocols.* Totowa, NJ: The Humana Press, 2004.

Folger, Tim. "The Next Green Revolution." *National Geographic*, October 2014. Accessed March 23, 2017. http://www .nationalgeographic.com/foodfeatures/green-revolution.

Harmon, Amy. "Golden Rice: A Lifesaver?" *New York Times*, August 24, 2013. http://www.nytimes.com/2013/08/25 /sunday-review/golden-rice-lifesaver.html.

McGuire, Andrew. "Agriculture Requires Fertilizer Inputs, and That's Good." *Perspectives on Sustainability*, CSANR, October 16, 2014. http://csanr.wsu.edu/agriculture-requires-fertilizer.

Nickerson, Cynthia, Robert Ebel, Allison Borchers, and Fernando Carriazo. "Major Uses of Land in the United States, 2007." U.S. Department of Agriculture, Economic Research Service, 2011. https://www.ers.usda.gov/webdocs/publications/eib89/11159 _eib89_2_.pdf.

Radiolab. *The Bad Show* (sound recording). June 4, 2012. http:// www.radiolab.org/story/180092-the-bad-show.

Regalado, Antonio. "As Patents Expire, Farmers Plant Generic GMOs." *MIT Technology Review*, July 30, 2015. https://www .technologyreview.com/s/539746/as-patents-expire-farmers -plant-generic-gmos.

Specter, Michael. "Seeds of Doubt." *New Yorker*, August 25, 2014. http://www.newyorker.com/magazine/2014/08/25/seeds-of -doubt.

Specter, Michael. "Seed Wars." *New Yorker*, November 2, 2012. http://www.newyorker.com/news/daily-comment/the-seed-wars.

Stewart, Neal C., Matthew F. Halfhill, and Suzanne I. Warwick. "Transgene Introgression from Genetically Modified Crops to Their Wild Relatives." *Nature Reviews Genetics* , 4 (2003): 806-817. doi:10.1038/nrg1179.

Van Eeenennaam, Alison L., and A. E. Young. "Prevalence and Impacts of Genetically Engineered Feedstuffs on Livestock Populations." *Journal of Animal Science.* 92 (2014): 4255-78. doi: 10.2527/jas.2014-8124.

INDEX

ABOUT THE AUTHOR

Katharina Smundak is a writer and English teacher living in France.

PHOTO CREDITS